A GIRL'S

GUIDE TO STOCK TRADING

EXPLORE SEVERAL STOCK TRADING OPTIONS THAT SUIT YOU

HOW TO BECOME A SUCCESSFUL STOCK TRADER WITHOUT A FINANCE DEGREE

DISCLAIMER

TABLE OF CONTENTS

INTRODUCTION

An Investment In Knowledge Pays The Best Interest – That's How I Started Out

HAVE FUN AND MAKE MONEY!

Hi gorgeous! I am Julia Goodman and you might already know me from my Fashion and Mommy blog https://www.JuliaJolie.com , my online TV Channel http://www.juliajolietv.com or my corresponding online store http://www.JuliaJolieBeverlyHills.com .

So yes, I am a Fashionista, Mommy to a little Toddler Girl and the total opposite of what you might consider a Stock Trader.

So, you might wonder: what in hell does SHE know about stock trading? Well, first and foremost, I am an entrepreneur and I love to empower women. I am somebody who likes to start businesses from scratch and show the world that it IS possible to establish a successful business with little resources and money. Same story with stock trading: It is a business and you don't need much money to start out!

ANY women can become a prosperous stock trader! All it takes is hard work and discipline!

In this book, I will show you exactly how to do it! And, you will have a fun-filled journey to making an astounding amount of money! All the girls out there who feel a bit alien in the financial markets should know that there is nothing to be afraid of! You do not need any financial education to navigate your way through the various stocks and understand how they work. All you need to do is to believe in yourself and not give up and trust me, you will make it!

"Everyone has the brainpower to follow the stock market. If you made it through 5th Grade Math, you can do it!"
-Peter Lynch (American Investor)

Knowledge; however, is quite essential. You must have some know-how of what you're getting yourself into!

I, myself, do not have a financial degree but I taught myself everything about the art of trading. It took a lot of blood, sweat and tears, but now I can consider myself a successful trader! And again, you don't need a lot of money to invest in stocks, I am the living example. I started out with only $3,000!!

How Did I do that?

I took a chance and invested all my $3000 in a futures contract of crude oil. (Unfortunately nowadays, these contracts are a little bit more expensive).

Crude Oil is the world's most actively traded commodity and I was instantly intrigued by it. Understandably, it was a rather risky investment but I still took the chance. What you should keep in mind, is that if the investment seems risky; do not invest excessive money into it. I had saved the $3000 to try out stock trading, so I was mentally prepared to lose it if I had to.

Only use the funds that you are sure won't be needed elsewhere. Investing all the savings that you may need for your retirement or your children's college fund is just not the wise option.

"Never invest emergency savings in the stock market"
-Suze Orman- Merrill Lynch Financial Advisor

Use the money that you received as a bonus from your job, or an incentive that came along at the last minute from a sale you were not expecting! So, even if you happen to lose it, you would not feel very miserable about it.

Another important thing that I did, and which worked just fine was that I stayed with buying just one contract of crude oil. I only used another contract, when I felt there was a need to 'average down'. I know, that you do not yet know what 'averaging down' is, but, if you keep reading, you will soon have a pretty good idea!

WHY SHOULD YOU CONSIDER IT SERIOUSLY?

You may be wondering: why is making an investment so important, when you can easily make income from a regular job? You are not entirely wrong. All your needs, including your conveyance, grooming and other household expenses can be taken care of through your salary. So why do you need this?

This is your back up!

Let's have a look at a few points that will show you for what!

- If you want to take a break from your job and take a vacation, the vacation you take will not be cheap. Your investments, however, will keep making you money while you are vacationing with your family in Cost Rica!

- You can always save the profits for the kids' college fun!

- You can even keep the profits aside for your retirement.

- The funds can also help you acquire assets you previously couldn't dream of! That car you had been dreaming about for years and that house that seemed just so perfect for your family could become very much affordable for you.

- A few extra dollars never hurt anyone!

- You are tired of your 9-5 job and want a new career

- You are a stay at home mom and want to make a few extra bucks

- You want to work from home

YOU CAN START SMALL

One thing that will make you very comfortable about making an investment with the stock market, is that you can start small if you want to. You don't have to invest thousands of dollars on a hunch! Even if you don't want to start out with a couple thousand, there is still a way to learn and practice stock trading. You can learn by paper trading (trading with fake money) or start out with Apps like Robinhood where you can trade with as little as $100!

Take your time, make small investments and if the result is great, you can start adding the zeros to the number of dollars you are using. Start with a few hundred dollars and be safe!

IT IS A REAL JOB?

Most people have reservations about stock trading as being something that's

a one-time stroke of luck or a fluke or chance. This is not true. The stock market is only a gamble for the gamblers. You need to be very disciplined to succeed in trading. You need to keep your emotions away. You

cannot trade to compensate for your losses. And you must have a trading plan. You can carry it on for the rest of your life like a job. But you need to make as much effort on it as you do with your job or your business and you WILL become successful with it!

IT BEARS GREAT FRUIT!

One of the most awesome things about stock trading is that, although it takes the same effort as needed in any job or business, it gives you returns ten times higher when compared with any profession or commerce. You can be a working woman, a single mother or a young entrepreneur looking to make your way through the sea of dominating men and you can stock trade as easily as you do your hair every morning! You can even stock trade from bed in your pajamas!

With stock trading, you have many options available to you. All you need is a little bit of confidence in yourself and a go-getter attitude that can conquer the world! Every girl can be a self-made boss of her own time if she wants to! You can do it too!

"How many millionaires do you know who have become wealthy by investing in savings accounts? I rest my case."
-Robert G. Allen- Motivational Speaker

CHAPTER 1

RISKS AND REWARDS

You will never know what you are doing in stock trading if you are unaware of the two main idols of trading: Risks and Rewards!

Stock trading is like a game that has an element of luck in it but for the most part, it is based on some very calculated risks

and bears very high rewards. You just need to understand your risk bearing capacity. Rewards will follow you automatically.

RISK

You simply cannot evade risk in life. It is involved in all kinds of decisions you take whether they are personal, professional or financial. So, why be afraid of a little risk in trading? Most people prefer to keep their funds in savings accounts in place of investing in stocks due to fear of losing their funds in a short period of time. But they fail to see that their funds are still at risk. Sure, they won't find them gone when they wake up the next morning but the saving rates that banks offer are far below the inflation rate.

So, in the end your expenses always end up being way more than your savings. It compels you to use your principal at some point in time. You still lose your funds eventually only at a slower pace than before!

There is this famous Trader, his name is Bruce Kovner. He believed in himself so much, that he borrowed $3,000 on a credit card and traded soybean futures. He was very lucky and this trade got up to $23,000! You know what he's worth now? $5.3 billion!!! Was it risky? Most definitely! But this $3000 investment changed his life! So why not try it out and see if it changes yours too?

Explore Your Risk Tolerance

Just because you can't evade risk completely, doesn't mean there is no way to reduce your risks. But before you try to reduce or manage your risks, you should think about what kind of investor you want to be. Some people are aggressive investors and have a high-risk tolerance which means, they can potentially gain higher rewards. However, I do not believe in high risk trades. High risk traders end up losing all their money sooner or later! Only invest 1%-5% of your funds and ALWAYS have a stop-loss order in place, which simply means that you put an order in place to stop you out when a trade doesn't go your way. That way, you WILL make money… slowly but steady…

"I have continually witnessed examples of people that I have known being ruined by a failure to respect RISK. If you don't take a hard look at risk, it will take you."

-Larry Hite- Hedge Fund Manager

Risk Factors in the Stock Market

Trading is always a bit risky and there are several things that might influence your trading and increase your risk. Some of these may have direct effects while others may be indirect and yet their power is great. Let's have a closer look at some of the factors that can potentially change your buying and selling decisions!

Liquidity of Equities

I know there are many things here that may seem a bit new to you, like 'liquidity' and 'equities' but don't you worry, I will make sure you get it all right!

So, first off, liquidity means the ability of your investment or equity to turn into cash. So, the sooner you can turn a specific equity into cash, the more liquid it is. The longer it takes you to sell it and claim

cash against it, the more illiquid it becomes! One of the best examples I had with illiquid securities is in options trading. Sometimes, with less popular option contracts, there's not enough volume, meaning not enough people are willing to buy off your contracts from you and you get stuck not being able to sell that contract, which expires after a certain date and you lose all your money!

Purchasing Power

The purchasing power is the maximum amount of money available to you to make trades. Most experienced traders trade with a margin trading account. With this type of account, you can borrow money from your broker. Which means you can potentially trade with more money than you have in your account! For example, if you had a margin account with $3,000 cash and your margin rate was 50%, then your total purchasing power would be $6,000! Here is a snapshot from my account. My net liquid is $239,735.16 but my stock buying power is $379,470.32!

Margin trading is a great way to enhance your potential returns and gives you the potential to do more trades, however, this is a riskier way of trading and if the trade doesn't go your way, there is a higher chance of loss and even a potential automatic sale of the security. The broker will make sure to get his money back! Therefore, I don't recommend a margin account for beginners.

Diverse Portfolio

You can choose to invest in one stock or you can decide to make an investment in different stocks. You can also invest in Options, Futures and Forex. Personally, I love options and futures. We will talk about the differences, advantages and disadvantages later in the book. Generally, investing in various securities is less risky. Ever heard the expression, 'never put all your eggs in one basket'?!

Decline in the Stock Market

The stock market can go three ways: up, down or sideways. Since the middle of 2009, we have been in a bull market, which means, the market has been going up constantly. Many people are wondering when the bearish market will start (decline in the stock market). One of the most common misconceptions is that you cannot make money in a declining market. This is simply wrong. As a trader, you learn to short a stock and there is no way to successfully trade without ever shorting. On a given day, any company, even the most successful companies like Google or Amazon, go up and down in the stock world. As a trader, you learn to predict the moves of a company, betting on the stock to either go

up or down. You don't have to worry that a company will go out of business, you can make $$$ on exactly that.

REWARDS

Your risk tolerance is also dependent on the rewards associated with any investment. If the investment has a nominal profit attached to it, you may consider pulling out your funds even at the slightest risk of loss. However, if the rewards are very high, it is a wiser option to wait or the losses to turn into profits! High rewards play a huge motivation to continue a high risk bearing investment.

Rewards can be in any particular form. Firstly, a reward of your investment is the profit you are making. Secondly, the company may give you Options as a reward. Thirdly, you also get paid Dividend against your shares.

Let's take a quick peek at the rewards you are entitled to when you buy stocks.

How to make a Profit from Trades

Our number one rule to making a profit is: Never buy a stock when it's high. It's like buying a Dior dress from the Summer Collection in June. It will lose its value IMMEDIATELY. There is a famous saying in the stock trading world: Buy the rumor, sell the news. It means that if you hear about a stock everywhere and everybody is buying it, you are most likely too late. The stock can plummet any minute and it is too risky to get in at that point. A smart girl will invest in a stock that nobody has heard of yet, but that seems promising. Stocks get pumped and dumped all the time. Don't be a sheep and follow the mass. Only the people who think for themselves make it in this business.

Number two rule: Always take the profit! Don't stay in the trade! No matter how experienced of a trader you are and how sure you are that the stock is going to go up more, get out and take your profit! A bird in the hand is worth two in the bush! Don't try to predict the stock market, take the money and run! Don't be greedy! The foremost reward of investments in stock trading is the profit that you can make from simply buying and selling stocks. Many people make the mistake of buying stocks when the prices are high. They are sooo wrong! You can't do it as a day trader! Like I said before, the only good time to buy a stock, is when its prices are low. Later on, when they will be on a rise, you can sell your shares and make a profit from the sale of the stocks itself.

You may be wondering, why anyone else would decide to buy shares at a time when even you won't prefer to do it? There are situations where buying shares at higher rates is actually. This is usually for big time

Investors. It all depends on the reason you are willing to buy stocks at an unlikely time.

For instance, you hold 1000 shares of a certain company. Those 1000 shares make 10% of the total share capital of that company. However, someone else owns 4100 shares of the company which makes 41% of the total share capital.

In this case, you may not feel very prudent in buying shares at a higher price but the person who holds 41% shares does. They just need 10% more shares to gain controlling shares of 51% in that company. They will definitely want to buy more shares even if it costs them more than its actual price.

In this scenario, you can make profit by selling your shares at a higher rate. The person who buys from you gets management rights in the company you have both invested in. This makes it a win-win situation for both the investors.

But now we're talking big money investments. Now we're talking Wall Street Money. So let's get back to our game plan: Making a little money every day and make a living stock trading!

Options

Options are another form of reward that you can avail when you invest in shares. Stock options are a little tricky to understand, however, they can be used as a great means to generate income. Options are actually one of MY favorite ways to make money in stock trading! In my opinion, it is less risky than future trading and you can start with a smaller amount of money… no need to dat trade options at this point. You can just hold on to them for days, weeks, or even months… and wait till the trade goes your way sounds easy, right? It

basically works the same way as buying and selling shares or future contracts… But, let's back up a minute, first you need to understand what options are.

Defining Options

Options are a **right** to buy or sell shares at a certain price (**Strike Price**) within a certain time period (**Before the Expiration Date**) that a shareholder can purchase or is rewarded from the company they have invested into. An option can also have a price. When the shareholder **exercises** (buys

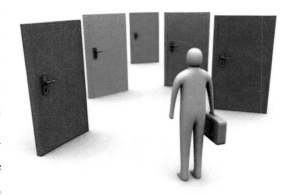

or sells shares using the option) their options they have to pay a certain **premium** (fee) for doing so. That's it. Let's clear that out first.

For instance, you can buy options of ABC Company at $5 or ABC Company gives an option worth $5 to you because you hold 10% of its shares as a reward.

Right and Obligation

Remember, options are a **right** not an **obligation**. You can choose whether you want to exercise the option within its expiration date or not. If you don't use the option it will become worthless after it expires. So, this way, you can actually buy an option of a company for much cheaper than the actual stock BUT still make an insane profit!

Call and Put Options

If you do exercise it, you can benefit from it greatly. You can either buy shares using the option you hold or you can sell shares using the option you hold. When the market price of the shares is greater than the strike price, you have to buy shares using options to make them worthwhile. When the market price is lower than the strike price then you need to sell shares using options to make them worthwhile. So basically, if you buy puts, you're betting for the stock to go down. If you are buying calls, you are betting for the stock to go up.

Let's take a look at an example.

Continuing the above example, for instance, ABC Company gives you an option worth $5 to buy or sell 100 shares at $10 per share within the next 30 days. During the next 30 days the market prices of the shares rises to $15 per share. The premium to exercise the option is $1.

Here, the option price is $5, the strike price is $10 per share, the market price is $15 per share and the premium to exercise the option is $1. Now, if you decide to buy 100 shares by exercising this option you can make the following amount.

$$=100*\{(\$15-\$10)-\$1\}$$

=$400

Woohoo! You made $400 by using options!

Likewise, if in the same scenario, the market price of the shares during the next 30 days goes down to $7 per share, selling your shares becomes a wiser choice. In this case you can buy 100 shares at the market price and sell 100 shares using your option at strike price ($10 per share) to profit from them.

=100*{($10-$7)-$1}

=$200

So here, you made a profit of $200 by using options!

Let's remember:

The option to buy is known as **call option**.

The option to sell is known as **put option**.

The Right Turns into Obligation

The value of an option which seemed constant in the above example ($5) also changes as the expiration date of the option gets closer. If the market price of the shares keeps rising during the life of the option, the value of the option keeps on increasing as well. So, you can also choose to sell the option when its price rises higher than what you had purchased it for. The tricky part here is to know when to sell your options. The closer you get to the expiration date, the riskier it becomes to keep it.

So sometimes you are down on a trade and need to make the crucial decision of whether you should be taking a loss or wait.. and see if the stock turns around and goes your way… remember, an option can also deteriorate and you can lose all the money that you invested… and this is when most people panic and don't know what to do!

The best thing to do is to buy your options with an expiration date way in advance. However, these options are less risky and this is why they are more expensive. Playing options is an art form! You need to watch the market carefully and have great intuition! And the most important thing of all: Never panic! Keep a clear head and make a rational decision! I know, it may look scary, if you see that you are down a few hundred or even thousand dollars on your trade! But carefully evaluate if it's worth to get out! Remember, the next day, the market can turn around and you might be in profit! You can't be emotional in this game!

So, in my opinion, Options are one of the most coveted rewards any shareholder can ask for! You can turn your losses into your profits quite easily if you know how to use your options.

DIVIDENDS

Dividends are a separate form of reward that a shareholder can receive from their investment in a certain company. Before we get to see what dividends are, you should know one thing. Only a few companies offer dividends. Many companies which are new and just starting out cannot pay out dividends. Companies which have been in business for many years offer dividends. Let's see how dividends are defined.

Defining Dividends

Dividends are paid out to shareholders from the **Net Profit** of the company. After determining its net profits, a company has two clear options. It can either re-invest the profit earned back in its capital or it can pay it out to its shareholders as a reward. The profit that the company decides to re-invest is called **Retained Earnings.** The profit that the company decides to pay out is called '**Dividend**'.

There is a certain percentage of the profit that shareholders get according to the number of shares they hold. For instance, if someone holds 100 out of 1000 shares of the company, they would get a different amount of dividend from someone who holds 500 shares of that company.

Every company has their own policy for paying out dividends. As an investor, it is important that before you choose any company, you take a look at their dividend policy. The amount and timing of payment of the dividend can vary according to the company policy. Some companies pay dividends quarterly as well as semi-annually. Most companies stick to paying out annually.

Let's have a look at the various types of dividends that a company can offer you if you choose to invest in it so you can make a better investment decision!

Dividend Payments that are Stable

Some companies provide stable dividends no matter what profits they are earning. For instance, the company defines a slab that shareholders who have between 1 to 100 shares will receive dividend of $50 every year. Here, whether the company makes profit of $1000 or $100, it will pay out $50 to all the shareholders in the defined range.

The amount of dividend in this situation remains stable whether the company makes higher profits or lower profits in any given year. Shareholders receive dividends irrespective of the profits that the company makes.

Dividend Payments that are Constant

In the case of constant dividends, the company makes a policy that it will pay a certain percentage of its profits to its shareholders every year. Here, the dividend varies every year according to the profits a company makes.

For instance, the company policy reads that if you hold 100 shares of the company you will get a dividend equal to 1% of the entire profit of the company every year. If the company makes a profit of $1 million this year your dividend equals $10,000 this year. However, if the company makes a profit of $500,000 next year, your dividend also drops to $5000. Here, the percentage of the dividend offered remains constant.

Dividend Payments from Residual Profits

Residual Profits are the amount that a company has left after it has collected retained earnings from the net profits. The residual profits are either divided equally or according to a certain percentage among the shareholders as per company policy.

For instance, if a company makes a profit of $1 million but decides to retain $800,000 into its capital, dividends would be paid out of only $200,000. The company can choose to distribute it equally among the shareholders or publish slabs to offer it as per the number of shares held by each person.

If you know exactly what the dividend policy of a company says before you choose to make an investment into it, you will know exactly what kind of income you will be able to generate from it besides buying and selling its shares. Dividend income can prove to be quite a life saver in such a case. You can use this extra money to buy more shares or you can save it for yourself!

CHAPTER 2

WHAT ARE STOCKS?

You may already know the answer to that. Of course, you see the news. You also read the newspaper. Many times you have heard conversations of your friends and colleagues when they are relentlessly complaining about the stock prices!

So, it is safe to assume that you know what stocks are. But are you sure you have the correct knowledge regarding them? Let's find out!

STOCKS:

Stocks are basically shares of a particular company that are available for public purchasing. Do all companies have shares? No. Only Public Limited companies have shares. These are the companies listed on the New York Stock Exchange. Is it that simple? Not really, but we can figure it out!

As an investor you just need to know the number of shares that you can buy from the stock market. To be exact that amount is called issued share capital of a company.

Authorized Capital

Ok! I know! It may seem a bit irrelevant and boring, but trust me, it's not. You must understand the nature of stocks in order to understand exactly how they work, otherwise you will find yourself in a big mess not knowing how to back track anymore. So, bear with me for a minute let's find out what authorized capital is!

When a public limited company first starts its business, it has to prepare a feasibility report. This report lists down everything that the company needs to initiate its business. After approval of this report, a long process begins for incorporating the company and commencing its business. But we don't care about that. In this report, among other things, the company states its authorized capital. This is the total number of shares that a company can issue during its life. However, it is not necessary that it ends up getting the exact number of shares as it has been authorized to receive. It can have a significantly lower number of paid-up shares and an even smaller number of issued shares. How does that happen?

Let's take an example to understand. For instance, a company is authorized to issue 1000,000 shares during its entire life. In the initial year of the business, the company feels it does not need a lot of resources so it chooses to release a public offering of only 500,000 shares. After a couple of years, the company feels short of funds and makes another public offering of up to 200,000 and so on until it uses up its limit of authorized share capital.

Now let's see what are paid up shares and what are issued shares!

Paid-Up Share Capital

We will look at this through the above example. For instance, the company has offered 500,000 but it receives money from shareholders for only 400,000 shares. In this case, the paid-up shares are 400,000 for which the company has received payment.

In contrast, if the company receives payment for 600,000 shares, the paid-up shares will be 500,000 shares only. The company will refund buyers of 100,000. So, now you know you can also be refunded sometimes when you try to buy stock! It's a very common practice so don't worry. It happens.

Issued Share Capital

These are the number of shares that the company finally issues to shareholders. When you buy stock, you are actually obtaining a part of the company's issued capital. You become entitled to rewards and a risk bearer of the company as well.

The shares you own carry their own risk and sometimes you also end up losing your principal. So, know exactly what you're getting into before you take one more step!

HOW DOES IT WORK?

This is another essential question. Stock trading is not as easy as it may seem. Yes, at its core, it is simply buying and selling. But several factors are affecting this trade. So, you need to be fully aware of all the factors in order to make a sound decision.

See, taking decisions, choosing carefully are the things that matter most in stock trading. You have to make choices that pull you from the brink of incurring a loss. How do you do that?

You analyze before deciding! Simple, isn't it?

Let's have a look at the two major ways of analyzing your decision-making.

Basic Analysis

In this type of analysis, you look at the factors associated with the investment company. For instance, you are looking to buy shares of XYZ

Company. First thing you can do is take a very close look at the financial statements of the company. Make sure, they are in good financial standing.

But here is what affects a stock on a day to day basis: the reputation that the company has! Read up a bit about the company. Most importantly; see, if there is news in the market about a major change in the company. For example, while searching about XYZ Company, you come across this article of the company's CEO that they will be retiring the next week or may be moving to another company. So what is likely going to happen? Investors will probably get scared because they don't know who is going to replace the CEO. The change in the decision-making management of the company is huge. Several factors are related to that. How would the new CEO of the company run things? Whether their decisions will seem sound to the Board of Directors? Whether their strategies will lead the Company to Profit? Or whether the company will sustain a huge loss because of the change?

All these questions arise with such an important change. And all of these affect the stock prices of any given company. So what will likely happen to the stock?

It will likely go down...So what should you do? Theoretically, you should short the stock or buy puts. However, be cautious: the price drop might have already been priced in, or you read the news too late! This is why stock trading is all about timing!

Technical Analysis

Technical analysis actually helps in making the decisions of buying and selling your stocks. Basically, in stock trading, the key to steady success is to know exactly when to buy stocks and when to sell them. Now, no one will tell you that other than the stock broker you have hired who is charging a high fee for his services. You can either pay them a fee incurring a large expense or you can work a little harder to find out suitable times yourself.

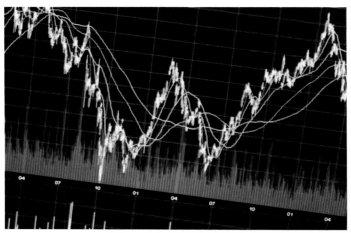

The reason your stock broker will accurately tell you the proper timing is the fact that he is well accomplished in reading financial, economic and other such factors affecting the stock market.

A technical analysis takes place through the following tools:

Charts

Charts represent a clearer picture. Every security you invest in has a stock price chart. Its price is shown by a moving line, called the **Trend Line.** The direction of the line determines whether it is a good time to buy or sell. You just have to identify what their directions mean.

For instance, you choose to invest in the securities of XYZ Company. The investment platform will show you a tab to see the stock price of the securities. As soon as you click on the tab, a chart will appear like the following:

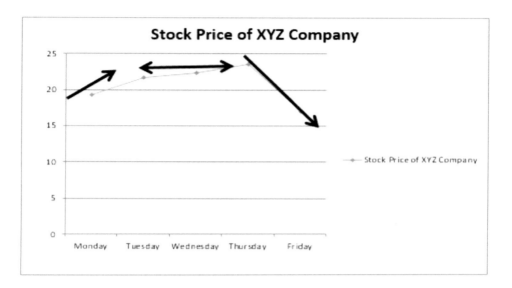

The above chart shows the stock prices of the XYZ Company during one week. If you want, you can also see the stock prices of the securities you are investing in for a month or even years. So, basically, these charts show you the historical prices of the stock that you want to invest in. You can choose if you want to see the 'trend' for the past week, month or year. It helps you predict the movement of price in future based on historical prices. The predictability of the future market prices becomes easier with the help of historical prices.

The above chart is showing historical prices of the stocks of XYZ Company for the past week.

The shape ⟷ represents the area of **resistance** in stock.

Let's consider another chart for the stock price of XYZ Company.

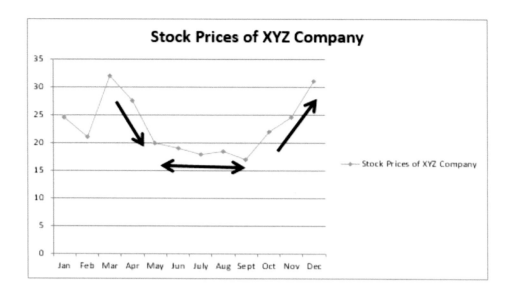

This chart is showing the historical stock prices of XYZ Company for the past year. During the past year this shape ⟵——————➤ shows the area of **support**.

Now let's find out what Resistance and Support are.

Resistance

This is an area where Investors get hesitant to go over. They stop buying. At that price point. Refer to the first chart to see that in the given week the stock prices are on a constant rise. In fact, they stay there for 3 days. That time period is perfect for selling because after that peak the stock prices will likely fall. Therefore, when in resistance, sell your stocks as soon as you can. A trend line that is constantly rising is called a **Bullish Trend Line**. It always leads to resistance. This is basically a rising trend.

Note: Of course, stocks break resistance! But, this is usually a big deal. If a stock breaks resistance, it will likely continue rising till the next resistance point.

Support

This is an area where you can buy more stock. Refer to the second chart to see that in the given year, stock prices are constantly going down. This decline takes place for 4 months and then suddenly prices rise up. So, if you are planning on purchasing the stock of XYZ Company, it is good to buy it at the bottom of the decline of the stock price, because trend shows that after a consistent decline prices will shoot up. So ideally, you buy at the decline and take your profit when it goes back up.

A trend line that is constantly declining is called a **Bearish Trend Line**. It always leads to support. This is basically a declining trend.

Therefore, getting used to the charts showing trend lines should be your first priority when you invest in stock. Keep checking the trend line every week, month or year to see when you can grab your opportunity to score big by selling at the right time. So when I play options, I usually look at the charts of the last week, sometimes a day, or even the last hour. You should check out different charts, depending if you're looking to day trade or swing trade.

Statistics

These are commonly known as technical indicators.

These indicators are different from charts. They are mathematical calculations that confirm your deductions about the rise and fall in prices. Just see the stock prices after these indicators have been applied to those on the stock exchange websites to see which indicator was able to predict your deduced price correctly.

For instance, you assumed that stock price for XYZ Company will be $22 at the end of April. However, the technical indicators show that this price is going to be $15. Here, your charts and statistics do not match. Does that mean one of these deductions is flawed? No, that just means that one of these calculations has taken into account factors that the other has overlooked. Buying the stock of XYZ Company at this time would be taking a risk since you can't predict the price right.

On the other hand if both the charts and statistics show the prices at the same level say $20, then you can safely purchase the stock and hope for a high return. At this point in time, you know what to expect for the foreseeable future.

The technical indicators can be of two types:

Leading Indicators

The indicators in this type simply show the stock price prediction before a certain event has occurred to bring about that change. For instance, taking the previous example of the change in CEO of XYZ Company if the stock prices are predicted to decline before the CEO has changed, that means this prediction was made using leading indicators. RSI, Stochastic, Parabolic SAR are a few of the leading indicators.

Lagging Indicators

These indicators confirm the drop in stock prices after the occurrence of an event that has caused the decline. For instance, continuing the above example, if the stock price falls after the CEO leaves, then it will mean that lagging indicators have predicted this price. Moving Average is a lagging indicator.

Technical Analysis simply allows you to make informed decisions about stock trading.

SELECT YOUR INVESTMENT EQUITIES

Now that you know how to determine the point in time in which buying and selling make stock trading profitable for you, you need to select the equities that you want to invest in.

The companies listed on the New York Stock Exchange are your potential targets. First you need to see the stock prices of each of the companies you are interested in. Then you should measure the risks and rewards as you have seen above that are attached to that company. Then you can choose to buy its stock keeping in mind the trend lines. If you feel that it is not the right time to buy stock for a particular company, just don't! Look for another potential investment. Never buy securities at a higher price. You never know how high it will go. What if it simply doesn't go any higher and you end up stuck with the securities for another year until it hits resistance again and you can finally sell. See my point? Try to go with bigger companies like Fang Stocks: Facebook, Amazon, Netflix or Google. These are the best known stocks and usually have high volatility and big news coming out weekly. This is great for Day- and Swing Trader! You need the market to be volatile to make money!

CHAPTER 3

IS A LARGE INVESTMENT MORE PROFITABLE? YES AND NO!

Stock trading is not as simple as it seems. However, that is no reason for you to worry! There are simply many aspects of it that you need to understand before you make an investment. So far, we have covered the basic points. Now you know a lot about stocks, their prices and the risks and rewards attached to them.

What's next?

Some people believe they can make only as much as they invest. The more the merrier! While this saying holds true for partying and having fun, it definitely does not apply to stock trading. You have to know when to stop. In some securities investing a large sum of money is wise. In other securities it is nothing short of foolishness. It all depends on the securities you are going to invest in and the factors surrounding it. In addition, it also depends on how much money you have and how much you should invest.

Now you need to know how much you are willing to invest in it. You have many options. You can invest a small amount to see if it brings in any profits before risking huge funds. Sometimes, making small investments end up in loss only because they were small. So, you need to know exactly how much to invest in which situation. This decision simply varies according to each individual so we will see some general factors.

EVALUATE YOUR OWN FINANCIALS

No matter what the market price of the stock, if you don't have enough money, you should just not invest into securities. What does that mean? Can only people with a large bank account invest into stock market? No. You  must have a clear idea about your own financial position. For instance, if you make about $1000 every month, should you have $12000 at the end of every year? No. Here, you are not accounting for your expenses.

In the same way, before investing check all your bank accounts and savings. Segregate your money for various purposes. There may be a wedding coming up in the family. Some renovations may be pending for your house or you may even be planning on buying a car in the next few months. Some of your savings will certainly go into expected expenses in times to come. Therefore, if you have savings of $10,000 in hand, you should only consider the amount of $5000 for investing in stocks.

Now you know your own limit. You can only buy stocks worth of $5000. At this point, it should be your aim to make further investments from the profits you retain from this amount rather than making more investments from your own pocket.

So, if you have larger savings in the bank and fewer expenses in mind for them for the foreseeable future then you can make a large investment. However, if you have limited savings in the bank then first you should calculate the expenses you may be facing in the next year and then use the savings in hand after accounting for those expenses. My Tip: Even if you have a lot of money to invest with, never invest all the money into one company! Spread it out! That way, if one of your stock trades goes south, you still have another chance with the other one!

ASSESS MARKET RISK

Market risk is another important factor in determining your investment amount. You need to know whether you need to invest large funds into your stocks or only a small amount can make good profits. For that, market risk is important. If the stock is risky you should try to invest small amounts of money into it at a time. If the stock is steady then you can put a little larger sum on the line.

CALCULATE BOTH LOSSES AND PROFITS

Whichever amount you select, always know the wager. Never underestimate your losses and overestimate returns. That's the biggest mistake you can make. See each of your investments both in terms of profits and losses.

For example, if you are investing $10000 in the stocks of ABC Company, evaluate that if stock prices rise, you will be able to sell stock worth $10k for $15k but never forget that there might be a chance that you will lose half or all of your money.

There is one way to prevent loss of all your funds. It is known as **stop loss order**.

STOP LOSS ORDER

"The key to trading success is emotional discipline. If intelligence were the key, there would be a lot more people making money trading... I know this will sound like a cliché, but the single most important reason that people lose money in the financial markets is that they don't cut their losses short."

-Victor Sperandeo

So, what is stop loss order? It's not very difficult to understand. If you like shopping, you will get it just right. Sometimes you get the "buy one, get one free" deal at the store. You take it even when it comes with the condition to pay a little extra, only because you want the free product.

For instance, you get the Victoria Secret Lip-gloss for $6 as it is. However, the store offers to give you another bottle of the lip-gloss, if you add another dollar into the mix. So, you are willing to bear the loss of $3 that you had not been expecting to spend today, but you do anyway because you are going to get an extra bottle worth $6.

This willingness to bear loss can be understood as stop loss order. Though, you don't get anything for free with it. You just get the loss part.

This willingness to bear loss can be understood as stop loss order. Though, you don't get anything for free with it. You just get the loss part.

It is an order by the shareholder to sell the stock, if its market price drops below a certain value. For instance, you are trading the stock of ABC Company. Currently, the market price of ABC Company stocks is $50. You set up a stop loss order at $49. This means that you are only willing to bear 2% risk of your full investment in ABC Company. Now, if the stock prices drop below $49, your stocks will be sold at the next available market price. Therefore, if the stock price falls to $48.5, it will be sold at that price and you will have to bear a loss of 3%. It is still 1% more than you expected. You were willing to bear 2% loss but now you have to bear 3% loss.

Sometimes, this loss can increase even more. This generally happens when the stock market closes above your stop loss order but over the weekend something happens that causes further decline in the price. So, when the market opens again on Monday the stock price suddenly drops.

Let's continue the above example. The stocks of ABC Company may be on $49 on Friday, but when market re-opens on Monday it falls to $45 and your stock will be sold as per your stop loss order. Here, you will have to bear 10% loss in place of your 2% anticipation.

Therefore, you should be careful when to apply the stop loss order. It prevents the loss of all your funds. This is usually a helpful tool in large investments. In such cases, a total loss becomes irrecoverable. But loss of a small amount can be compensated easily.

DON'T THROW IN EVERYTHING AT ONCE

Large investments are a really good choice, if you like high risk trades and are pretty certain that it will go the direction that you are anticipating. You only want to invest large amounts if it's a quick day trade or a very long investment. Stock prices of any company can vary at any point in time

and it is the timing that matters. The company should be a secondary consideration. For instance, you have $5000 that you have to invest in a company that will give you high returns.

This is a large sum of money. You have to be careful here. You have two options. You can either invest all $5000 in the stocks of ABC Company, or you can start with $1000. If you throw in all the funds at once and unfortunately the stock prices decline, you will suffer a loss. If you start with a smaller amount you will be able to observe the trend of the prices of the stock of ABC Company. If you feel that trend does not seem highly profitable then you can create a stop loss order for the sum invested and explore other stocks for investing the rest of your money.

Therefore, always consider these factors before deciding how much money you want to invest into which stocks. Your good luck charms may be working, but stock market runs on way more than on luck!

CHAPTER 4

FIGURE OUT YOUR TRADING STYLE: FIND OUT WHAT YOU'RE GOOD AT

Well, this is the point where you are really exploring yourself, to know what kind of a girl you are! It's like finding out, whether you are a glamorous babe or a cute romantic! Only here you will be looking at how you prefer to trade.

The trading style you choose shows who you are. It takes into account the types of securities available for trading. It considers your willingness to go as far as you can. It includes your risk bearing capacity, your fears and your anticipations. Sometimes, a trading style suits you, but you are using that particular style for a type of security that doesn't work in that kind of trade, or is simply too risky!

You know a few securities by now, like stock and options but there are other securities that may seem suitable to you according to your situation.

The trading styles simply help you seek out what you are best at. Once you embrace your own trading style, you will be quite comfortable in trading in multiple securities without hesitation.

There are basically 3 trading styles that you can adopt. Each of these works for everyone differently. Don't undermine any of these. Go through each of the styles carefully so you can find your strengths and weaknesses. Once you know what you can do best, all you have to do is take the first step!

DAY TRADING

You have heard me talk about day trading a couple of times in this book already. I simply love day trading! Day trading can be defined as the buying and selling of securities in a single day. The trader taking part in this form of trading does not take an overnight risk. The securities that you can invest in while day trading are highly liquid. These securities can be bought and sold before the close of business on the same day. The most common places for day trading are foreign exchange markets and stock trading markets.

Some people might say, this is high-risk trading but I highly disagree! I think it is way more predictable! Yes, you have to be on you're a-game and very sharp, but you can also make a lot of money! Let's have a look at a few of the factors that make this type of trade so volatile and fun!

Sharp Price Movements

Do you remember the trend lines above? The changes in those trends took days, weeks and months. Those charts belonged to securities held for a long period of time. However, in day trading trend lines change within minutes and hours. This is called a sharp movement of stock prices. This means that your reaction to the change in stock price must be as quick as the change itself. What does that mean? Well, basically, your **order execution** to buy or sell must be on time. We'll see what an order execution is in a minute.

This sharp change in price can create a loss for you if you lose the opportunity to react accordingly. As a day trader, it is essential that you have your eyes on the trend lines of your securities all day. Any small movement in prices can prove to be a difference maker for you. It can mean that you make thousands or loose thousands. Let's have a look at it with an example.

For instance, you buy 100 shares of ABC Company worth $10,000. A couple of hours after the market opens, the market price of the shares rises from $100 to $104 per share. In this scenario, if you can sell all your shares at this point, you will be able to make a profit of $400 today.

100*104 = $10,400

10,400-10,000 = $400

If you don't act fast, the prices can decline after another couple of hours. So, you have to give an order execution to sell your shares immediately.

Order Execution

As apparent from the name, an order execution basically means that you have placed the order to buy or sell your shares in the stock exchange. The order execution is an important factor, as it is directly related to other important elements such as time and rates. Let's see an example to better understand this idea.

For instance, you place an order to buy 100 shares of ABC Company which are currently at the market price of $20 per share. This makes the total value of the shares at $2000 at the moment. However, by the time your order gets filled the price per share has in increased to $20.10 per share. This means, that now you have to pay a total of $2010 for the same amount of shares as before. You are paying $10 extra for a little delay in the order filling. Why does the delay happen?

Well, order execution is just not as simple as going to your favorite store and buying your favorite pair of shoes! It's a tad more complicated than that. What do you think happens when you place an online order to buy the shares that seem suitable to you? Do you think it works just like ordering something over the internet? The stock market doesn't really work like Ebay!

So, you must be wondering, what's the difference between placing an order to buy your favorite handbag from Ebay and placing an order in the stock market for buying shares of ABC Company?

See, on Ebay, the product you have ordered is available for sale immediately. Once, you place the order at a specific price, that price won't change. The order is placed in just one click, directly from the Ebay website, which is connected to the retailer who is selling that particular product. However, when you place an order in the stock market for shares, it is not immediately placed. Because the trading website you are using is not connected with the stock market directly. It doesn't matter which website you are using. All websites are connected with stockbrokers. And in order for you to buy some shares, somebody else needs to sell them. So this might take some time.

High Liquidity of Securities

Another reason, day trading is highly risky is because the securities are highly liquid. They can be turned into cash easily. In this case, all it needs is one false decision and your entire investment can suffer a loss. You have very little room for mistakes. High liquidity brings changes in stock prices almost every hour. You have to learn to keep up your pace with these abrupt changes.

More Investments by Large Financial Institutions

You may not have an idea about these, but most of the large financial institutions make an investment in Day trading. There is a very good reason for that. Day trading is quite risky, it needs a large amount of capital to justify its high risk nature and it needs access to a **trading desk**. We'll see what a trading desk is in a minute. The important point at this time is the fact that, large financial institutions prefer investing in day trading.

What does that mean for you as an individual day trader? For starters, these large financial institutions become your direct competitors! This can be bad news for you, if you are not too quick on the uptake. Look at it this way. Day trading is an ocean. You have to share this ocean with the big sharks (large financial institutions). In such a case, what are your chances of survival? What is so hard about competing with the large institutions?

Well, to begin with, a large financial institution can invest a large amount of money and is also quite capable of losing it without being damaged too much by the loss. If, unfortunately, you suffered a loss, you will have a hard time recovering from it.

Another important factor is that large financial institutions hire hundreds of individuals to day trade with their money. So, basically, you are not against one organization, you are against a hundred individuals. If you look at it this way, you have a chance at making as much profit as each of the individuals hired by financial institutions do! So what is the best strategy to compete with these big fishes? Exactly! Go with the flow! Don't swim against them! If you see a lot of buying power, go buy as well. If you see a lot of selling going on, it's probably best to short the stock as well.

To sum it up: You must be way more vigilant while day trading, when compared with any other type of trade. But you can also make way more money with it.

Involvement of Trading Desk

In the world of trade and commerce, some things are just quite literal. Yes, a trading desk is actually a desk on the trading floor on New York Stock Exchange. What does it do? It takes orders from individuals like you and I. They also take orders from large financial institutions. There are different trading desks for different types of securities.

For instance, there will be a separate desk for foreign exchange securities and a different one for income based investments such as government and corporate bonds. Each desk has its own fee for taking orders from individuals and financial institutions.

A trading desk is simply that channel that can execute your orders instantly. However, they charge a high fee for their prompt services. That is why larger financial institutions can afford day trading easily.

Investment of a Large Amount of Money

So here is the bad news about day trading: Money plays a huge factor!. Legally, you can only start day trading with a minimum of $25,000. Anything less, is not allowed. So obviously day trading is for more advanced traders, because you should NEVER start trading with so much money, if you don't know what you are doing!

But how can you practice day trading?

1. You can always start paper trading, which is trading with fake money to get the gist of it. That way you won't lose actual money.

2. You can trade with futures. For example, a Crude Oil Futures Contract costs around $6000 and you can start trading with one… with futures, you can buy and sell whenever you please. Within seconds, minutes, hours, or days! That way, you can practice your day trading strategy, without having to invest $25,000.

DAY TRADING AS A JOB

You can make a lot of profit from day trading if you treat it as a job. Just ask my husband! However, it is very high pressure work and you need to concentrate all the time, so this is not for everyone! You have to be very disciplined or you will never make it. Discipline is the divider between people that say it is gambling and people that actually make money with it!

What I usually do, is I trade a couple of hours in the morning and then I am done for the day! This was one of the main things that attracted me to trading. I can make money for a couple of hours and have time for my daughter, my other business "Julia Jolie Beverly Hills", my hubby and my friends. So you tell me, is there a better way to make a living than this?

SWING TRADING

So depending on the opportunities of the day, I go back and forth between Day Trading and Swing trading. So, what's the distinction between the two? The only difference: The stock that has been purchased in swing trading must be held at least overnight. You are not allowed to sell it on the same day, before the close of market.

Swing trading is great when you start out. It is not as stressful and time consuming, because you usually stay in the trade for a couple of days, weeks or even months. So, if it doesn't go your way, you can keep the stock and wait for a change of direction.

Keep in mind, when I talk about swing trading, I talk about swing trading with Options. Otherwise you still need a $25,000 minimum, which we want to avoid at the start.

Small price movements play a significant role in swing trading as well. Traders generally look for ways to make big money by moving their stock with sharp changes in prices.

For example, you hold 100 shares of ABC Company currently at a market price of $25 per share. You buy a couple of Options for this stock.

If you are swing trading these shares, you have to first study the trend lines of at least a few days before, so you make a decision to sell. If in the previous few days, the charts show you a declining trend which seems to be rising slowly since this morning, it might not be too wise to sell right now.

However, if despite the declining trend in the past few days, you can see a rising trend in the last 24 hours and you have seen a similar spike in prices in one of the previous days then you should consider selling. It is risky, seeing the volatility of the stock but then that's what swing trading is all about. If you feel unsure, observe the movement of the trend lines for a couple of hours more before taking a decision. It will help you make up your mind accurately! Remember, it is always hard to predict the stock market and there is no strategy that works 100% of the time.

Firm knowledge of technical analysis and a clear understanding of the trend lines, charts showing bullish trends and bearish trends is a must, if you want to swing trend successfully. These are the same trends we have discussed above so you don't have to worry. They're quite easy to follow, once you get the hang of them!

There two main factors to consider while swing trading. You have to keep an eye on the **downside risk** and **position sizing** of your stock.

Downside Risk

This is basically an estimation of the amount of risk of loss that an investment carries. It shows how much loss an investor would have to bear if a particular investment turned bad.

For instance, if you are currently holding 100 shares of ABC Company, 200 shares of XYZ Company and 300 shares of QWY Company you are responsible for all 600 shares. You will be entitled to receive profits from each of these securities and you are the risk bearer in each of their cases. However, do all three of the companies' shares have the same potential to create loss for you? Looking at this example, if you had to choose one company that had the least potential to create financial loss for you, which one would you pick?

If you asked me, the ABC Company has the least potential among these companies as you only hold 100 shares of this company. This potential, that the 100 shares of the ABC Company carry, this is called your downside risk. So, actually, you are bearing a total risk of 600 shares from all 3 companies but these particular shares can cause you loss to the extent of 100 shares only. This extent of loss is the downside risk.

In swing trading, you have to consider each of your investments carefully and consider which one has the maximum or minimum downside risk so you can act upon the sudden movement of price correctly. With perfect estimation for loss, you can easily capitalize on your gains from each investment individually. The pool of your investments will become even bigger because of your particular attention to each of the securities you own.

SWING TRADING VS DAY TRADING

With so many similarities, it is essential to see how swing trading is different from day trading. Day trading closes on the same day and it generally refers to charts of technical analysis spread over a few hours in a business day. In contrast, in swing trading stock must be kept overnight. However, this does not refute the fact that swing trading is preferred by many of the day traders as it is easier for them to keep an eye on the stock movement.

So, if you trade at home and you have the time to keep your eyes on the technical analysis charts for the most part of the day then swing trading can bring you large profits!

INVESTMENTS

In the stock market, stock trading and investment are quite different. Generally speaking, difference may not be that evident. However, when you look at these two concepts, they are quite different from one another.

Trading basically denotes a buying and selling activity. Let's take an example to understand that. You bought 100 shares of ABC Company for $10 per share. So far, this is only the buying part of the trade. In the next couple of hours, the market price of the shares drops to $8. At this point, you may be thinking that your investment may be as good as drowned. However, if you are day trading, you have until the close of the day to determine whether your investment is fruitful or not.

In another hour, the prices shoot up to $12. Here, you decide to sell your shares immediately. Finally, your shares are sold at $11.5. This is the selling part. In this instance, your trade is complete and you have made the following profit.

$$= \{100 * \$11.5 - 100 * \$10\}$$

$$= \$1150 - \$1000$$

$$= \$150$$

Here, you have made a profit of $150 from trading 100 shares of ABC Company.

Investments are more **buying and holding** types in nature. This holding is for an extended period of time. It can be for a year or more at a minimum. This holding works regardless of the hourly, daily, weekly or monthly change in stock prices.

Buying and Holding

This is a strategy used by many investors. The benefit of this long-term investment is mostly that the investor doesn't have to worry about any short-term changes in the market price of the stocks. The holder of the investments is only concerned with the accumulated profits at the end of their holding tenure. The fluctuations in the market price of the stock taking place on a daily, weekly and even monthly basis become redundant to investors with long-term holdings. They just need to see the progress in their profits each year. Keeping an eye on the stock prices every day or week or month becomes unimportant.

For instance, you buy 100 shares of ABC Company for $10 per share on the 1st of June this year. Here, the buying part of the transaction is done. Now, you have to hold the shares you have bought until 1st of June next year. On the 2nd of June this year, the company suffers a major loss and the market price per share drops down to $5 per share. Will you sell your shares at this point to cut your losses? In case of investments, you actually don't sell your shares until a designated period of time. During this time period, the stock price can fluctuate as many times as possible. It will impact the ultimate profits of the shareholder. If the prices have been on a declining trend throughout the year, at the end of which the shareholder will be able to retain profits and their principal amount, their profits may be significantly lower than initial estimates. Sometimes, they might even lose part of their principal if the company's position keeps declining.

However, if during the year the company gets back on an inclining trend then the entire situation can change. The important thing in investments is to notice consistency in the rise and decline of stock prices. If you are

54

observing a consistent decline in prices and nearly 3 quarters of the year have passed, at this time it is highly unlikely that the trend will begin to rise again. In this scenario, you can pull your money out and cut your losses.

Generally, in case of investments, companies get back on the rising trend unless they suffer an irreparable loss, like losing a key management personnel or a getting hit by a natural disaster that compromises the stability of the company.

Management of Investments

Investments are managed by different companies and individual brokers. You can select the person you are most comfortable with and allow them to manage your portfolio of investments. They will keep an eye on major changes in the prices on your behalf. You won't have to look into it yourself. In exchange, you will be a charged a small fee by the company for their management services. This is generally the case with Mutual Funds' investments.

Investments are more of a passive form of activity to generate wealth through stocks. This passive investment is preferred by many people. You can try these too but if you are looking to score big in a short span of time without wanting to gamble in a casino, trading should be your first priority!

CHAPTER 5

LOOK FOR THE INVESTMENT EQUITIES THAT GO WITH YOUR STYLE!

Once you have established your particular style of trading, you have to take the next big step in the cycle of trade. You have to find out which equities are meant for your attention and which you should ignore at all costs! See, there is a reason when they say to each his own. You just can't be good at everything. Vice versa, you can't be bad everything either. So, you have to determine, which equities make you a star and which will dump you quite far away from the financial markets.

You can only pick suitable equities after you have understood the various styles of trading and investments. Why? Because now you know which game is your best. Now all you have to pick are the major players. Each equity jives with a different style of trading. Therefore, whichever style you choose, you have to trade in the equities that go with that particular trading style. Let's find out which equities are best for which trading style. Everybody has their favorite stocks that they like to trade. Once you choose, study them every day and get to know their movements. Some stocks are very volatile with high risk, high reward, others move slower and safer. Some stocks are cheaper, some more expensive. Choose at least 5 stocks that you always keep an eye out on. You can't trade only one stock every day, some days there are just no good moves so you need to trade a different stock. This is why you have to keep an eye on a couple of them.

STOCKS

Let's address the elephant in the room first of all. We know what stocks are and how they work. We have also seen many ways of trading stock.

Stocks which constitute the biggest set of equities that an individual can invest into are the most compatible with two styles of trading. You can use stocks in both day trading and swing trading. In either case, you have to monitor the fluctuations in the short-term market prices of the stock. The only difference between the two is that, if you choose to use day trading for stocks, you have to initiate your investment with a minimum of $25000.

This is a huge amount, to begin with, especially if you are very new to trading. In addition, day trading holds a lot more risk than swing trading. So, if you choose to invest in stocks, pick day trading only if you have more than $25000 for investment. In fact, only if you have at least double that amount. If $25000 is all you've got as your total savings of the past years, then the better option for you is to consider swing trade.

In swing trading, you won't have to invest $25000 in one go. You can start as small as you like so you can get a feel for how trade actually happens. It is also a good choice to start with, if you are simply looking to try out a few new things. Once, you understand how the trend lines work and when you should buy and at what time it is prudent to sell, that's when you can pitch in completely. It will not only give you a sense of safety regarding the money you have invested ,but it will also help you observe the rise and fall of stock prices overnight, a few days and even few weeks. This knowledge can also sharpen your skills for day trading.

Keep in mind, just because you invest money in your trading account, doesn't mean that you have to use all the money to trade. In fact, try to only use 5% of your total investment on each trade. It is never smart to risk more money than that.

FUTURES AND OPTIONS

These are the next equities that you can choose to invest in. In fact, I only trade futures and Options, as I mentioned before. Why? Because even if you have at least $25,000 to play with, you will get much higher profits and returns on futures and options than stocks. Stocks are much more expensive, so unless you are investing for the longer term or have a $1 Mio trading account, there is no point trading the actual stocks!

Let's take a deeper look at these.

Options

Options are the right to buy or sell shares, on a fixed price, during a specified period of time. We have already seen how options work in the above sections..

For example, if you buy an option to purchase 100 shares of ABC Company at $25 per share within a period of 30 days for $10 on 1st July, you are allowed to hold this option until the close of 31st July. During this period, you can either exercise this option or sell it to someone else. Now, if the market price of the shares of ABC Company rises to $40 by 29th July, the value of the option will also rise from $10 to as far as a $100, because whoever will own it next will be able to save $15 per share if they exercise the option to buy shares of ABC Company. Therefore, you can make a ton of money with option trading with a relatively small investment..

On the contrary, if the market price of the stock reduces below the strike price of the options, the market price of the option itself reduces as it nears its expiration. So you have to sell at the right time or the option deteriorates and you lose your money. Again, it's all about the timing here!

Futures

Now this is an interesting concept and one of the best strategies for day trading. You know by now that day trading, although very profitable is rather a high risk trading. Well, in my opinion, future trades are the riskiest types of trades but also the most profitable. Remember, when I told you at the beginning of the book that I started trading with $3,000 and grew it to $25,000 to start day trading? Well, I did it with futures trading!

Futures contracts are an actual contract between a buyer and a seller in respect of a particular commodity, for a fixed price and to be executed on a specific date. These came into existence to accommodate commodity traders. For instance, ABC Company wants to buy 100 barrels of wine from XYZ Company. They both form a futures contract for the 100 barrels at $10,000 to be executed on July 31st. Now, in this scenario, even if the prices of the barrels rise to $12000 on 31st July, XYZ Company is obligated to sell the barrels to ABC Company at only $10,000 due to the futures contract. This futures contract has a price for which the ABC Company can sell it to QWY Company. If the ABC Company bought the futures initially at $500, then by the time the prices of the wine barrels will rise, the value of the futures will also rise to almost a $1000, because whichever company will use this contract, can buy the barrels by saving $2000 according to current market price of the wine barrels.

The futures contracts were meant to hedge prices of commodities for businessmen so they could avail discounted rates.

So, how can you as a day trader use futures to your advantage? It's quite simple.

Continuing the above example, you are not interested in buying the wine barrels but you can buy the futures contract any time before 31st July. The good news for you is that the second the price of the wine barrels increases; you can sell this contract to a potential buyer for a higher price. Therefore, this is one of the best profit-making trades in day trading.

One thing that you have to be aware of: generally, futures contracts are very volatile and if you don't keep your eye on them for a minute, you can lose everything. The problem with futures trading is that you basically play with "borrowed" money and if the trade doesn't go your way, you get a so called "margin call" to either deposit more money or the broker automatically liquidates your trade and you have to take a loss. This is why future trading is only for the clear headed girls that are willing to watch the market very closely and are able to execute smart decisions without overthinking them!

INVESTMENT

These are one of the most stable equities to buy. Investments are long-term and they generally comprise of Mutual Funds. . As you have seen before that in case of investments, you do not need to worry about immediate or short term changes in the market price of the stocks. As a result, these are very safe as you look back for their profits after years and collect the profits when they ripe!

Mutual funds are very easy to invest into. You only need to have a bank account and the money to invest. There is no need to monitor the stock and absolutely nothing at all to do but wait until the maturity of your investment to collect profits! However, these profits are usually very low so you won't become rich anytime soon, unless you invest a substantial amount of money.

"Money is just something you need in case you do not die tomorrow. Let this is a reminder for you not to obsess over profits and losses. In whatever you do, strive for enjoyment, focus, contentment, humility, openness... Paradoxically (and as an unintended consequence) your trading performance will improve significantly."
— *Yvan Byeajee, The essence of trading psychology in one skill*

CHAPTER 6

DAY TRADING STRATEGIES FOR YOU: ENTRY & EXIT POINTS

Beyond all the trend lines and technical analysis, day trading can be extremely easy to execute. However, you cannot plan to succeed without viable strategies. You need a few of these to survive as a day trader. When you are day trading on a daily basis, then it becomes a must that you achieve some level of expertise while doing it. These strategies will help you gain that expertise. There will come a time when you won't have to try and remember any of these strategies. You will be using these out of practice!

Let's take a look at these strategies or rather the steps to your success as a day trader.

DECIDE HOW MUCH YOU WANT TO INVEST

The first move is to know how much you are willing to bet on any particular trade. Evaluate all the shares available for trade and determine how much each of these deserves your investment. This decision can be based on the trends that each of the stocks move in. For instance, while comparing stocks, you can feel that betting a larger amount in the shares of ABC Company is a much better option when compared to investing in the shares of XYZ Company. Any wrong estimation here can lead to very different outcomes for you. So, decide prudently about how much money goes where.

PICK: OPTIONS, FUTURES, STOCKS ?

The next step is to pick the right equities for investment. As you have seen above, options and futures are some of the best things to trade in my opinion. Making an investment in these can lead to very high profits. Your skill in identifying what you like to trade best.

FACTORS THAT SHOW MINUTE PRICE MOVEMENTS FOR BUYING

There are some factors that you can clearly see affecting the market prices of stocks. If you keep these factors in mind, you can easily overcome any potential losses and make day trading decisions that will always end up giving you profits. Let's see what these factors are.

Liquidity, Volatility & Trading Volume

Liquidity

We have already seen what liquidity is. What's important is that what it does for you! Due to liquidity, you can enter and exit a stock at a very good price. You can easily understand how to use price **bids** and **ask price** of a stock. You can also understand how to benefit from a low **slippage**. You can easily see how to benefit from **spreads** in a stock. All these lead to a good buying and selling decision, giving you better profit-making opportunities. You can also find your advantage in the difference between the expected and the actual price of a stock.

Bids are the prices that a buyer can offer to buy a particular stock. Each buyer places their own bid. The seller has the opportunity to select the best bid for his stock. If a stock has higher liquidity, higher number of people would be bidding on that stock. In addition, you can bid the price that you can afford. In this way, you can get the stock for the price that you want! **Ask Price** is the minimum price that the seller of a stock will accept from his buyer. If there will be a lot of bids for a stock, the seller will be able to pick the best price for his stock. However, when there will be fewer bids and unfortunately, none would seem satisfactory to the seller, then the seller can set the ask price of his stock.

Let's see an example. For instance, 3 bids have been made to buy the shares of ABC Company. One is for $20 per share, another is for $21 per share and the last one is for $22 per share. However, the ABC Company can sell its shares for a minimum of $25 per share. In such a case, the ABC Company will release the ask price of $25. The interested buyer will then make their bid according to the best price of the seller.

Slippage is the difference between the expected price of a trade and the price at which the trade is actually executed. This difference can be a result of the delay in placing the order or due to any other situation during which the price of the stock increases or decreases.

Spreads are the difference between the bid price and the asked price. Based on spreads, you can make material decisions related to buying a security. Trading spreads is another great way to make money. But it is more advances, so I will keep this for our next book.

Volatility

The more volatile a stock is, the better for trading. Volatility brings chances of higher profits for a shareholder. For instance, you buy 100 shares of ABC Company at the market price of $20 per share at 10.am on 2nd of July. You were expecting the prices to rise by afternoon that day. Instead the prices fall to $18 per share. This does not mean that you have suffered a loss, not until the close of the day at least. Then, by 2.pm, prices rise to

$24 per share. Now, you know how volatile the prices of these shares are. Maybe in the next two hours the prices might drop again. So, at 2.pm you have a window of opportunity to sell and make a profit of about $4 per share. Now, what would have been the better play here? You could have anticipated the fall of the stock and shorted it at 10am. By 2pm you could have switched directions and bought the stock again. Or, in my case, I would have bought puts first (option trading) and after that calls. That way you could have made double the profit in the same time.

But in general: When purchasing shares, people who like to make quick and big profits go with shares having volatile market prices.

Trading Volume of the Shares

If the shares of a company are traded in a high volume on a daily basis, this means that there is a lot of interest in these shares. This is why you always want to trade stocks and options with a high volume. They move much better and you have better chances of making a profit.

IDENTIFY THE RIGHT ENTRY POINTS INTO THE MARKET

Once you have understood how to buy, you need to know when to buy. To be precise, you need to know, at which point it is wise for you to enter into a trade. This entry point is determined by many factors. Generally speaking, just watching the news can help you. Your timing is everything. So, keep yourself updated about the stock you are interested in buying.

Strategies for Selling

Another important strategy is knowing WHEN to sell the stock. Let's have a look at popular selling strategies:

Trailing Stop Order Strategy

We have previously seen how stop loss order works. So, you know how to save yourself from loss. However, trailing stop loss orders helps you exit the market by cutting your losses and sometimes even making you a profit.

Trailing stop loss is very similar to stop loss, however it works in an automatic way. In trailing loss you have to set a specific percentage to stop your loss. If the stock price goes below that percentage, the stock will be sold automatically. For instance, you buy 100 shares of XYZ Company for $20 per share. At that time, you place a trailing stop that if the market price of the shares goes below 20%, then, it should be sold. Imagine that in the next couple of hours the price of the stock moves up to $25 per share. Although, this is good news, if you are dealing with volatile stock, you know that the prices might come crashing down any second. At this point, you can set your trailing stop to 10%. In this way, if the price of the stock went below $22.5 per share, your stock would sell, making you a profit of maximum $2.5 per share. By using this strategy, even if your stock prices decline, you will make a profit.

Profit Target Strategy

This is one of the best exit strategies. You can set the profit targets when you buy a stock. So, when the market price of the stocks reaches that target point, it automatically sells. For instance, you buy 100 shares of XYZ Company for $20 per share. If you set that you would like to sell if the stock prices rise up to 20%, then the moment the market price of your shares reaches $24, your stock will automatically sell out and you will be able to leave the market with profits.

Day trading is no piece of cake, even if you have eyes on the screen all the time to monitor the fluctuation in market price of your stock. However, if you know the strategies to buy a stock, identify its entry point and you can easily set up its exit point then you can be a successful day trader working without a flaw.

CHAPTER 7

DAY TRADING STRATEGIES FOR YOU: TECHNICAL TOOLS IN DAY TRADING – RSI

Patterns don't work 100% of the time. But they are still critical, because they help you define your risk. If you ignore patterns and focus on hunches, feelings, and hot tips, just forget about achieving consistency.
-Ifan Wei

There are many strategies and patterns that can lead you to become a successful day trader. Not all of these strategies are based on theoretical tools. Many of these are based on technical tools. These tools can assist in your day trading activities, so that you can determine your entry and exit points into a stock easily.

RSI: RELATIVE STRENGTH INDEX

The RSI is an Indicator, a Pattern to predict where the stock is going to move. Now this is a very technical tool, but you don't need to worry. It runs on very simple principles. These principles are known as "overbought" and "oversold". When you know what these are, you will be able to understand exactly how the RSI can help you in day trading.

Basically, a stock can go into either **overbought** or **oversold condition**. This conditions indicate that a stock has gone to far into one direction and will likely change its direction soon. The RSI usually moves between 0 to 100.

Overbought is the position of the stock for a period of time in which its price is constantly moving upward. Traditionally the stock is considered overbought if it has an RSI over 70. It usually indicates that the stock is going to sell off soon.

Oversold is the position of the stock for a period of time in which its price is constantly moving downwards. Traditionally the stock is considered oversold when it's below 30 and usually indicates that Investors are going to come in and start buying soon.

How does it affect you? Well, lets look at an example. For instance, you are looking forward to buying 100 shares of QWY Company for $10 per share at 9.am on 3rd of July. Now, by 10.am the market price of the shares decreases to $9. You decide to wait until it drops further and sure enough by 11.am it goes down to $6. Now, this trend is obviously favorable for you.

So, the question arises, how to enter the stock at the right time? Or rather which is the right time? Well, look at the RSI! You need to understand when a stock is overbought and oversold.

RSI is the tool that shows clear overbought and oversold positions. Simply put, it has a scale from 0 to 100 that makes things very clear. According to RSI, if a stock is overbought, the RSI should be above 70. Likewise, if a stock is oversold, the RSI should be below 30. You have to remember these figures. Now, is this enough? Nope.

You should buy the stock when RSI goes below 30 and then returns back above 30. That's your entry point. You want to make sure that the stock is done dropping before you enter your position. In the same manner, you should sell the stock when RSI goes above 70. That's your exit point. Now, can you be a 100% certain that a stock will switch the direction from just looking at the RSI alone? No, of course not! That would be way too easy! But you gain an understanding that there should be a direction switch soon and it can help you make a wise Investment decision.

CHAPTER 8

DAY TRADING STRATEGIES FOR YOU: TRADING THE NEWS, REVERSE A TRADE & AVERAGING DOWN

You have seen several day trading strategies so far. But let's look at a couple more! I want you to k now as much as possible about the stock market and trading strategies! I want you to be as much prepared as you can be!

So let's have a look at these strategies and what they can do for you!

TRADING THE NEWS

Trading the news means that the trading decisions you are taking, are based on the news. Here, it becomes very important that you keep your eye on any and every news that comes out about the company that you're buying stocks from.

This news can be of several types. Let's have a look at the two broader types.

Recurring News

This is the kind of news that affects the stock prices of the company by occurring on regular basis. It includes news about changes in interest rates on a monthly basis or the issuance of earnings report every 3 months. What this means is that everyone is aware that this news will come out soon and it may have some implications on the market prices of stocks of that company.

Trading Earnings Reports

News traders, a high number of whom are day traders, benefit a lot from trading earnings reports. What are earnings reports? Every 3 months or quarterly, a public company releases its earnings reports for the past quarter. It either shows a percentage of increase in the profits of the company or a decrease when compared with the last quarter. Either situation affects the stock prices of the company. If there is a significant increase in the earnings of the current quarter then the stock prices are likely to rise as well. Likewise, if there is a drop in the percentage of profits then the stock process could also drop.

Trading news and earnings reports is a lot of fun and you can make a lot of money, because the stock usually has a huge price jump or drop. You just need to be on the right side, otherwise you can also suffer huge losses. So this trading style is definitely for my girls that don't fear risk!

One-Time News

This type of news is unforeseen, but it still helps you in taking a wise decision. It generally has a negative effect. It can be anything from news about a natural disaster to news about a terrorist attack on the company in question. Obviously, this one is hard to predict, unless you have some friends working for the press and hear it very early on.

REVERSE A TRADE

This day trading strategy is not very easy to execute but if you know about it, you can prevent loss of funds in certain cases. Traders tend to use it in Futures Trading, when seconds can mean the difference between a huge loss or gain.

When you push the reverse button, the trading software automatically sells your futures contract and buys in the opposite direction. So let's say you're in a Natural Gas futures trade and you bought 2 futures contract, because you think it will go up. Minutes after you see, that Natural Gas is selling off like crazy. You don't want to lose all your money and you're certain, the selloff will continue, because you just heard bad news in the Natural Gas sector. So you quickly press the Reverse Button and boom! You're trading in the right direction now.

AVERAGING DOWN

This is one of the strategies that day traders use most of the times. What this strategy entails is that the cost of stocks can be averaged down. How? Well, first off all, when you are averaging down, you are actually buying additional shares of the same stock at lower prices. Let's take an example here.

For instance, you have bought 100 shares of ABC Company at $30 per share. You were willing to buy 100 more for the same price. However, your luck turns in your favor (finally) and the share price drops to $20 per share. You proceed to buy the rest of the 100 shares as well at the reduced prices. So, now, your price per share for 200 shares of ABC Company would be as follows:

= $30+$20

= $50/2

= $25 per share

Although you bought a 100 shares at $30, the average cost you incurred for buying 200 shares was $25 per share, lower than the price for which you bought half the shares. Now, when you sell these shares, your cost price would not be $30 per share, it would be $25 per share.

One mistake that many Traders do, is averaging down when they're already in a losing position. You want to average down when you're certain, that the trade is going your way. Otherwise you just invest more money into a bad trade and risk losing even more.

CHAPTER 9

BEWARE OF THE MARGIN CALL

You have learnt several tools and techniques so far to make you a successful day-trader however you must beware of the federal laws involved in trading. If you overlook the federal laws, you will suffer way more loss than you had been able to make profit.

One such law is regarding the margin call. I have been talking about the margin call earlier in the book, but let's take a deeper look!

I have only experienced margin calls in futures trading, and wow! They are stressful!

A margin call is based on the federal law that every trader has to maintain 25% of equity in his trading account. **Equity** is the amount which is solely owned by the trader, it has not been borrowed from anyone. Why is there such a law? Traders borrow money from the brokers to make an investment. The federal has placed a limit on the borrowed amount.

So, what is margin call? If a trader has equity in their trading account which is less than 25% then the broker would call the trader to add additional funds into their trading account to meet the requirement of 25%, so they can adhere to the federal law.

Let's take an example, for instance you have $10,000 in your trading account. You want to buy shares of ABC Company which are worth $20,000. You borrow $10,000 from your broker to buy all the shares. Now, your trading account has $20,000 but you have equity of only $10,000 in your account. The next day, the value of the shares drops to a total of $14000. In this case, your remaining equity drops to $4000 which makes 20% margin. In this case, the broker will call you to add $1000 into your account so you could meet the 25% margin requirement.

If you fail to comply with the call, then the broker would have to sell some of your assets to reimburse the $1000 back into your account. So, keep your eye out for the margin call and be wary of the troubles it carries.

CHAPTER 10

CHANGE YOUR MINDSET

Trading is all about your mind and how you handle difficult situations. You have to be calm and rational to be a good trader. I think that is why we ladies have the better chances of being exceptional traders! We can be more calculated than men and not let our emotions cloud our judgement.

DON'T BE AFRAID TO FEEL FEAR

Most traders fail because they fail to address the fears that are haunting them. Try getting through your fears instead of running away from them. Face your fears head on!

DON'T BE GREEDY

Greed always takes down the best of traders. Most people can't stop, once they see that they can make money with it. Greed will always take you down in the stock market!

DON'T LET FATE CONTROL YOU

Many bad things happen that we end up calling as fate or ill fate sometimes. However, sometimes, we make uninformed decision leading to ill-fated incidents. You can control your fate. Keep presence of mind, stay updated with the current news and you can do just about anything even if it seems quite impossible! There is no fate in the stock market! There's only actions! I believe in each and every one of you! You can make it in the trading world! You don't need to become a professional day trader. Just use the stock market like an ATM machine. If you need to make some extra money for some new toys for your kids, then trade! If you want to start up your own business and need some capital, then trade! This is your opportunity to take destiny in your own hands and make any dream you ever had possible!

So, trade away girls and be the boss of your own destiny!

Xoxoxo,

Julia Jolie

Made in the USA
Las Vegas, NV
18 November 2021

34713571R00052